Ecumenical Services of Prayer

Consultation on Common Texts

Paulist Press
New York/Ramsey

Copyright © 1983 by Rev. Dr. Horace T. Allen, Jr., as prepared by the *Consultation on Common Texts.* All rights reserved. No part of this book may be reproduced or transmitted in any form or by any means, electronic or mechanical, including photocopying, recording or by any information storage and retrieval system, without permission in writing from the Publisher. Library of Congress Catalog Card Number: 82-60757 ISBN: 0-8091-5180-4 Published by Paulist Press, 545 Island Road, Ramsey, N.J. 07446. Printed and bound in the United States of America

The Publisher gratefully acknowledges the use of the following materials:
The English translation of the Lord's Prayer, Canticle of Zechariah, and the Canticle of Mary were prepared by the International Consultation on English Texts. The English translation of Psalms 123, 126, 136, 141, and 150 © The Grail (England) 1963 and published by Collins, (continued on page **62**)

Contents

Foreword   1

Introduction   3

    Morning Prayer ... 11

    Brief Order of Prayer ... 29

    Evening Prayer ... 37

Appendix   53

    I. Psalms for Morning, Afternoon and Evening   53

    II. Supplemental List of Psalms, Lessons and Hymns   61

Foreword

The Consultation on Common Texts (CCT) has been in existence since the mid-1960's as an informal forum for consultation on worship renewal between many of the major Christian denominations in the United States and Canada. This consultation has been concerned primarily, though not solely, with the progress being made by the member Churches in the reform of their liturgical texts and rites.

At present, participants in the CCT include persons from the following Churches or Church agencies: the Christian Church (Disciples of Christ); the Episcopal Church; the International Commission on English in the Liturgy (Roman Catholic); Lutheran World Ministries, representing American Lutherans; the Presbyterian Church in the U.S.; the United Church of Canada; the United Methodist Church; the United Presbyterian Church in the U.S.A.

In addition to serving as a means of consultation, the Consultation on Common Texts has sponsored several projects. The CCT initiated the project entitled "Prayers We Have in Common," which sought to provide a contemporary and ecumenical English translation of prayers in regular use by the Churches. After the CCT joined in the creation of ICET, the International Consultation on English Texts, these prayers became a part of ICET's work. An early psalm project led to *A Liturgical Psalter for the Christian Year,* which was prepared and edited by Dr. Massey H. Shepherd, Jr. with the assistance of the CCT and published jointly by the Augsburg Publishing House and The Liturgical Press in 1976.

This booklet, *Ecumenical Services of Prayer,* is the result of a desire expressed by various members of the Consultation on Common Texts to have a simple resource for worship in common on those occasions when Christians of various traditions gather for meetings or celebrations of an ecumenical nature. It contains a collection of prayer services and texts which were selected from or inspired by the worship books and traditions of the participating Churches. These services draw upon the ancient and enduring Christian practice of praying at certain times of the day.

Special thanks are owed to the worship specialists who were appointed by their Churches to serve on the project committee which prepared this collection. They are:

> *The Rev. Dr. Hans Boehringer,* Lutheran
> *The Rev. John Gurrieri,* Roman Catholic
> *The Rev. Dr. Hughes Old,* Presbyterian
> *The Rev. Philip Pfatteicher,* Lutheran
> *The Rev. Dr. William Martin,* Episcopalian
> *The Rev. William Wade,* United Methodist

In 1978 the Consultation on Common Texts began a project having to do with the lectionary (the cycle of Scripture readings for use at public worship). Most of the Churches in North America are at present using three-year lectionary systems that are strikingly though not altogether similar. In order to achieve even greater unity in worship, the CCT appointed a special committee and charged it with the task of harmonizing denominational variants in the lectionary for the Sundays and major feast days of the Christian year. The committee was also to make recommendations regarding calendar divergencies. This project was completed in early 1982. The CCT has commended it to the Churches for a period of trial use and study ending December 1, 1986, at which time the CCT will subject it to further review before final submission to the Churches.

Introduction

Finding Jesus at prayer, the disciples asked: "Lord, teach us to pray. . . ." He entrusted them with a form of prayer which was not only to become the prayer most frequently offered by Christians, but also a model on which much of Christian prayer in the future would be based. The "Lord's Prayer" is the Christian's prayer because the Church is always at one with its Mediator, who intercedes for it at the throne of the Father. The Church at prayer testifies to "the more excellent ministry" of the Lord Jesus, Mediator of a Covenant established in his own blood, "high priest of the good things which have come to be" (*Hebrews 8:6; 9:11*). Prayer is an activity which engages the whole person in praise, thanksgiving, adoration, and intercession, and which joins the person with the prayer of the whole Church and that of Christ himself.

The Tradition of Daily Prayer

The Churches of both East and West have never limited prayer either to the services of Word and Sacrament or to private piety. From earliest times Christians gathered at stated times of the day, especially in the morning and evening, to offer praise to God, to seek the intercession of the Redeemer for the needs of the Church and the world, and to ask for personal needs.

The first Jewish–Christians imitated the piety of their Lord, who was regularly found in the synagogue and Temple on the Sabbath and for the daily services of prayer. They continued to participate in the morning and evening sacrifices of the Temple, and they gathered in every corner of Palestine and the Diaspora for the daily liturgies of the synagogue. Even when the Temple was destroyed, and when greater numbers of Gentiles were evangelized and converted, Christians—Jewish and Gentile alike—continued the practice of daily prayer at various hours of the day.

The *Didache,* a second-century work rooted in the Jewish tradition of prayer, enjoins Christians to recite the "Lord's Prayer" three times daily. Even though Cyprian of Carthage (third century) affirmed that "for Christians there are no hours when they ought not concern themselves with frequent and continual adoration of God," Churches nevertheless saw the need to gather the community at specific times of the day to pray as an assembly. The *Apostolic Tradition* of Hippolytus of Rome (c. 215) encouraged all to gather regularly for instruction and to pray in the morning when the sun arose and at evening as the light of day faded. For Hippolytus, as for a constant stream of Christian writers and preachers, every hour of the day had Christological significance, uniting the believer with a particular aspect of the mystery of the Lord's life, death, and resurrection. Each and every prayer uttered was seen by them as the prayer of Christ himself.

Frequent Prayer—A Daily Cycle of Praise

"Praying always and never losing heart" (*Luke 18:1*)—these words inspired Christians to create a variety of forms of daily prayer. Out of the Jewish tradition of prayer, and in imitation of Jesus Christ, men and women prayed in their local churches in the morning and in the evening. They stopped work in their fields or shops to pray at the stated times. Others went out in the desert to pray alone. Still others created communities of prayer in which the challenge of continual prayer (*Ephesians 6:18–19*) expressed itself in a daily round of work and prayer throughout the day, and even through the night.

Christian piety in the Middle Ages was greatly influenced by the monastic experience of daily prayer, so much so that lay communities imitated prayer forms and accepted prayer texts from the monks and nuns. Originally the prayer of the laity, this daily cycle of praise or "prayer of the hours" became increasingly the task of "professional" Church members, clerics and religious who were officially deputed to pray on behalf of the entire Church.

Recovery of Communal Daily Prayer

Although the sixteenth century was a time of intense liturgical revival, not only with regard to the proclamation of the Word, the Eucharist and other rites, and of daily prayer, it was not until the late nineteenth century in Europe and the twentieth century in America that the communal and ecclesial renewal of daily prayer was effected. Although the intervening three or four centuries saw many attempts on the part of various Christian communions to reform the practice of daily prayer of the hours, these attempts failed either because of the continued centrality of the role of the clergy or because of the dominance of new forms of piety which were at once personal and individualistic.

The Roman Catholic Church has recently produced *The Liturgy of the Hours* (1974), a four-volume source of daily prayer; the Inter-Lutheran Commission on Worship has published the *Lutheran Book of Worship* (1978), which includes morning and evening prayer, as well as orders of prayer for other times of the day and night; the *Book of Common Prayer* provides Episcopalians with traditional forms of morning and evening prayer and also contains alternative offices; United Methodists are in the process of developing alternative series for daily prayer not contained in *The Book of Worship;* the 1970 *Worshipbook* of Presbyterians includes orders for morning and evening prayer, and a joint task force has been established to study the question of corporate prayer in the life of the Church, with a view to developing materials for use in its daily prayer life.

The impulse in each effort has been the same: renewing daily prayer by means of an examination of the early sources, with a view to gaining a more comprehensive ecclesial sense. Similarities are to be found in all of the books already mentioned: the use of intercessions; the assignment of the Canticle of Zechariah (*Benedictus*) to morning prayer and the Canticle of Mary (*Magnificat*) to evening prayer; the character of the hymns and their themes; the use of the Lord's Prayer both in the morning and in the evening; greater use of the Scriptures; and, lastly, a traditional course of psalmody.

A liturgical unity of a kind has already been achieved in the separate, although not unrelated, reforms. They point to new possibilities, some of which can be achieved now. This book is one fruit of those reforms.

Ecumenical Services of Prayer

Liturgical unity is not textual unity, any more than liturgical reform is synonymous with textual reform. The fact that Churches may use the same psalter does not necessarily mean that they pray together. Unity is an experience, a common experience, and liturgical unity is a common experience of common prayer. If the texts and structures of the books for daily liturgical prayer are similar, the actual experience of praying together is not necessarily taking place. This book, which is the result of common research and writing by the member Churches of the Consultation on Common Texts, attempts to answer the need and the challenge to experience daily prayer together.

The present volume does not seek to replace the liturgical books of any Church; rather it is composed for use at those times and on those occasions when Christians of different Churches gather to pray. It brings together elements of the different traditions of Christian prayer and synthesizes them in a common office which may be celebrated at ecumenical assemblies, for example, during the week of prayer for Christian unity, on Thanksgiving and other national holidays, at ecumenical clergy days, during inter-church council meetings, etc. It may also be useful in Churches which do not as yet have liturgical books with services of daily prayer and for private gatherings of Christians of various traditions.

Notes on the Use of the Book

Drawing as it does on Episcopal, Lutheran, United Methodist, Roman Catholic, and Presbyterian traditions and sources, this book will present its users with both the familiar and unfamiliar. It is, nonetheless, the result of discussion and research into the common Christian tradition.

A glance at the Table of Contents will show that the book is divided into four major parts: Morning Prayer, a Brief Order of Prayer, Evening Prayer, and the Appendix. The Morning Prayer section provides a full form of prayer for the morning hour. It is particularly characterized by its use of the *laudate* psalms (Psalms 145–150) and the comprehensive set of intercessions. The Brief Order of Prayer is designed especially for the beginning or end of meetings at various times of the day. Although it requires less time for planning and celebration than the services of Morning Prayer and Evening Prayer which are included in this book, it nevertheless provides a form of worship which is more truly liturgical and communal than the brief dedicatory prayer which often accompanies many meetings. Several choices are to be made before its celebration to ensure that it adequately reflects the time of day in which it takes place (morning, afternoon, evening). Evening Prayer constitutes the third major section of the book. This makes possible a solemn celebration of the evening hour and is distinguished especially by the light service with which it begins and the traditional use of Psalm 141. The fourth and final division of the book is the Appendix. This contains a limited selection of psalms for use in the three forms of prayer already described. These are divided within the Appendix according to the times of day during which they may be used. The Appendix also contains a supplemental list of psalms, lessons, and hymns for use at various times of the day, during particular liturgical seasons, and with special themes in mind. Although these materials are not actually contained in the book, they are listed here as an easy reference for using other resources. Throughout the book the psalms are given according to their Hebrew numbering.

 The collection of psalms and hymns is limited in order to restrict the bulk of the book. In this way it is hoped that the character of these hours of prayer, along with their elements and use, will be easily comprehended. The additional psalms in the Appendix make possible several distinct celebrations of each hour, a number which should be adequate for the kinds of ecumenical gatherings of one to two days for which this work has been developed. It is also hoped that those who use this resource will soon master it and then have recourse to other collections for additional psalms and hymns.

The arrangement of the services and the number of musical compositions contained in this book show a clear preference for sung celebration. In this way, the beauty and rhythm of the particular hour of prayer is able to emerge more completely, and the whole person is engaged in the experience of communal worship. Space was also a factor, since printing both texts and texts set to music would have increased the size of the work considerably. If, due to lack of musical competence or other reasons, there is a desire simply to recite some or all the elements of a service, this is usually possible with musical compositions by concentrating on the text alone.

The book is self-contained in every respect except with regard to the Scripture lessons. It is assumed that a Bible will be readily available in most gatherings of an ecumenical nature. The lesson may be chosen from an existing lectionary or for a special purpose which is the occasion of the gathering. A limited number of suggested lessons is found in the last section of the Appendix.

Various liturgical gestures and actions are indicated in the rubrics. These are merely suggestive and could be expanded or adapted. If the congregation seems uncertain about these matters during the service, an indication or invitation from the leader will help to provide smooth transitions between the various elements of prayer. Silence at appropriate moments, for example, between the psalms and after the reading, should be carefully encouraged.

These services assume the presence of a leader and at least one or two assistants. These assistants share the various leadership functions, such as leading song, reading the Scripture lesson and common intercessions.

The following table provides an overview of the structure of these services.

Morning Prayer	**Brief Order**	**Evening Prayer**
1. Invocation	1. Opening	1. ⎡Light Service⎤
2. Hymn	2. Hymn	2. ⎣Hymn ⎦
3. Psalms	3. Psalm(s)	3. Psalms
4. Reading	4. Reading	4. Reading

5. Canticle of
    Zechariah
6. Prayers of
    Intercession
7. The Lord's
    Prayer
8. Benediction

5. Prayer
6. The Lord's
    Prayer
7. Blessing

5. Canticle of Mary
6. Prayers of
    Intercession
7. The Lord's
    Prayer
8. Benediction

Morning Prayer

1. Invocation

The service begins with a formal or informal procession of leader and assistants. All stand as they enter. The leader begins the verse from Psalm 105 and the people make their response. The leader proclaims the prayer, to which all respond.

O give thanks to the Lord,
    call on his name,

**Make known His deeds among
    the peoples!**

Almighty and most gracious God,
    Creator of every family and nation,
We praise you that we have been called together as your people,
    set apart and baptized in the name of Jesus your Son,
    washed and ever renewed by your Holy Spirit.
Help us bear the image of Christ,
    and follow Him in our life together,
and grant that being truly your people
    we may be witnesses to your great faithfulness.

**All glory be to you, O Father,
    through the Son, in the Holy Spirit
    one God for ever. Amen.**

2. Hymn

O Come and Sing Unto the Lord
IRISH C.M.

3. Psalms

One or more of the following psalms may be sung or said. Musical settings of psalms 145, 148, and 150 may be found *in the Appendix. These may be used with or without the psalm prayers which appear with them. If they are simply recited, the "Glory to the Father" may be said after each psalm or after all have been completed.*

Psalm 145

I will exalt you, O God my King,
 and bless your Name for ever and ever.

**Every day will I bless you
 and praise your Name for ever and ever.**

Great is the Lord and greatly to be praised;
 there is no end to his greatness.

**One generation shall praise your works to another
 and shall declare your power.**

I will ponder the glorious splendor of your majesty
 and all your marvelous works.

**They shall speak of the might of your wondrous acts,
 and I will tell of your greatness.**

They shall publish the remembrance of your great goodness;
 they shall sing of your righteous deeds.

**The Lord is gracious and full of compassion,
 slow to anger and of great kindness.**

The Lord is loving to everyone
 and his compassion is over all his works.

**All your works praise you, O Lord,
 and your faithful servants bless you.**

They make known the glory of your kingdom
    and speak of your power;

**That the peoples may know of your power
    and the glorious splendor of your kingdom.**

Your kingdom is an everlasting kingdom;
    your dominion endures throughout all ages.

**The Lord is faithful in all his words
    and merciful in all his deeds.**

The Lord upholds all those who fall;
    he lifts up those who are bowed down.

**The eyes of all wait upon you, O Lord,
    and you give them their food in due season.**

You open wide your hand
    and satisfy the needs of every living creature.

**The Lord is righteous in all his ways
    and loving in all his works.**

The Lord is near to those who call upon him,
    to all who call upon him faithfully.

**He fulfills the desire of those who fear him;
    he hears their cry and helps them.**

The Lord preserves all those who love him,
    but he destroys all the wicked.

**My mouth shall speak the praise of the Lord;
    let all flesh bless his holy Name for ever and ever.**

Glory to the Father, and to the Son, and to the Holy Spirit:

as it was in the beginning, is now, and will be for ever. Amen.

Psalm 146

Hallelujah!
Praise the Lord, O my soul!
    I will praise the Lord as long as I live;
    I will sing praises to my God while I have my being.

Praise the Lord, O my soul!

Put not your trust in rulers, nor in any child of earth,
    for there is no help in them.

Praise the Lord, O my soul!

When they breathe their last, they return to earth,
    and in that day their thoughts perish.

Praise the Lord, O my soul!

Happy are they who have the God of Jacob for their help!
    whose hope is in the Lord their God;

Praise the Lord, O my soul!

Who made heaven and earth, the seas, and all that is in them;
    who keeps his promise for ever;

Praise the Lord, O my soul!

Who gives justice to those who are oppressed,
    and food to those who hunger.

Praise the Lord, O my soul!

The Lord sets the prisoners free;
the Lord opens the eyes of the blind;
    the Lord lifts up those who are bowed down;

Praise the Lord, O my soul!

The Lord loves the righteous;
the Lord cares for the stranger;
> he sustains the orphan and widow,
> but frustrates the way of the wicked.

Praise the Lord, O my soul!

The Lord shall reign for ever,
> your God, O Zion, throughout all generations.
> Hallelujah!

Praise the Lord, O my soul!

Glory to the Father, and to the Son, and to the Holy Spirit:

as it was in the beginning, is now, and will be for ever. Amen.

Psalm 147

Hallelujah!
How good it is to sing praises to our God!
> how pleasant it is to honor him with praise!

Praise the Lord, O Jerusalem! O Zion, praise your God!

The Lord rebuilds Jerusalem;
> he gathers the exiles of Israel.

Praise the Lord, O Jerusalem! O Zion, praise your God!

He heals the brokenhearted
> and binds up their wounds.

Praise the Lord, O Jerusalem! O Zion, praise your God!

He counts the number of the stars
> and calls them all by their names.

Praise the Lord, O Jerusalem! O Zion, praise your God!

Great is our Lord and mighty in power;
    there is no limit to his wisdom.

Praise the Lord, O Jerusalem! O Zion, praise your God!

The Lord lifts up the lowly,
    but casts the wicked to the ground.

Praise the Lord, O Jerusalem! O Zion, praise your God!

Sing to the Lord with thanksgiving;
    make music to our God upon the harp.

Praise the Lord, O Jerusalem! O Zion, praise your God!

He covers the heavens with clouds
    and prepares rain for the earth;

Praise the Lord, O Jerusalem! O Zion, praise your God!

He makes grass to grow upon the mountains
    and green plants to serve mankind.

Praise the Lord, O Jerusalem! O Zion, praise your God!

He provides food for flocks and herds
    and for the young ravens when they cry.

Praise the Lord, O Jerusalem! O Zion, praise your God!

He is not impressed by the might of a horse;
    he has no pleasure in the strength of a man;

Praise the Lord, O Jerusalem! O Zion, praise your God!

But the Lord has pleasure in those who fear him,
    in those who await his gracious favor.

Praise the Lord, O Jerusalem! O Zion, praise your God!

Worship the Lord, O Jerusalem;
    praise your God, O Zion;

Praise the Lord, O Jerusalem! O Zion, praise your God!

For he has strengthened the bars of your gates;
    he has blessed your children within you.

Praise the Lord, O Jerusalem! O Zion, praise your God!

He has established peace on your borders;
    he satisfies you with the finest wheat.

Praise the Lord, O Jerusalem! O Zion, praise your God!

He sends out his command to the earth,
    and his word runs very swiftly.

Praise the Lord, O Jerusalem! O Zion, praise your God!

He gives snow like wool;
    he scatters hoarfrost like ashes.

Praise the Lord, O Jerusalem! O Zion, praise your God!

He scatters his hail like bread crumbs;
    who can stand against his cold?

Praise the Lord, O Jerusalem! O Zion, praise your God!

He sends forth his word and melts them;
    he blows with his wind, and the waters flow.

Praise the Lord, O Jerusalem! O Zion, praise your God!

He declares his word to Jacob,
    his statutes and his judgments to Israel.

Praise the Lord, O Jerusalem! O Zion, praise your God!

He has not done so to any other nation;
> to them he has not revealed his judgments.
> Hallelujah!

Praise the Lord, O Jerusalem! O Zion, praise your God!

Glory to the Father, and to the Son, and to the Holy Spirit:

as it was in the beginning, is now, and will be for ever. Amen.

Psalm 148

Hallelujah!
Praise the Lord from the heavens;
> praise him in the heights.

Hallelujah!

Praise him, all you angels of his;
> praise him, all his host.

Hallelujah!

Praise him, sun and moon;
> praise him, all you shining stars.

Hallelujah!

Praise him, heaven of heavens,
> and you waters above the heavens.

Hallelujah!

> Let them praise the Name of the Lord;
> > for he commanded, and they were created.

Hallelujah!

He made them stand fast for ever and ever;
> he gave them a law which shall not pass away.

Hallelujah!

Praise the Lord from the earth,
> you sea-monsters and all deeps;

Hallelujah!

Fire and hail, snow and fog,
> tempestuous wind, doing his will;

Hallelujah!

Mountains and all hills,
> fruit trees and all cedars;

Hallelujah!

Wild beasts and all cattle,
> creeping things and winged birds;

Hallelujah!

Kings of the earth and all peoples,
> princes and all rulers of the world;

Hallelujah!

Young men and maidens,
> old and young together.

Hallelujah!

Let them praise the Name of the Lord,
> for his Name only is exalted,
> his splendor is over earth and heaven.

Hallelujah!

He has raised up strength for his people
and praise for all his loyal servants,
    the children of Israel, a people who are near him.

Hallelujah!

Glory to the Father, and to the Son, and to the Holy Spirit:

as it was in the beginning, is now, and will be for ever. Amen.

<u>Psalm 150</u>

Hallelujah! Praise God in his holy temple;

Praise him in the firmament of his power.

Praise him for his mighty acts;

Praise him for his excellent greatness.

Praise him with the blast of the ram's-horn;

Praise him with lyre and harp.

Praise him with timbrel and dance;

Praise him with strings and pipe.

Praise him with resounding cymbals;

Praise him with loud-clanging cymbals.

Let everything that has breath

Praise the Lord. Hallelujah!

Glory to the Father, and to the Son, and to the Holy Spirit:

as it was in the beginning, is now, and will be for ever. Amen.

All may be seated.

4. Reading

A lesson from Scripture is read. Before doing so, the reader may say:

A reading (lesson) from _____.

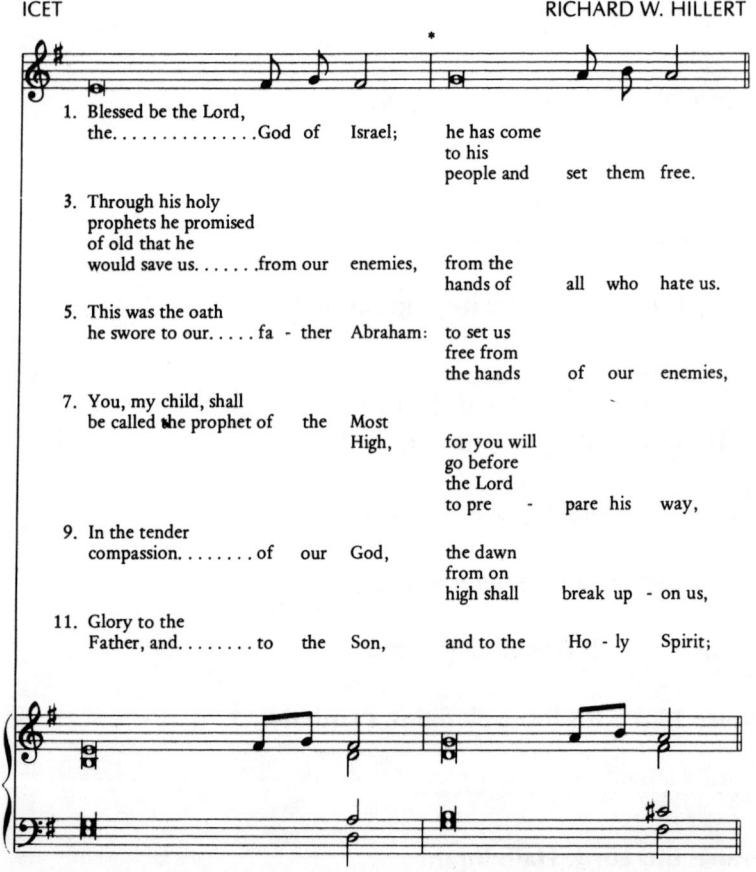

After the reading, the reader may say:

The Word of the Lord.

Thanks be to God.

Silence after the reading is recommended. A brief homily may also be given.

5. Canticle of Zechariah (Luke 1:68–79)

The Canticle of Zechariah is sung or said, in unison or responsively, verse by verse. All stand. (see opposite page for verses 1 and following)

6. Prayers of Intercession

The intercessions may be offered in these or similar words. Names of particular Churches, pastors, bishops, countries, presidents, etc., should be supplied as appropriate. Each intercession may be followed by a time of silence. All remain standing.

God of glory, and Father of our Lord Jesus Christ,
    whose name is blessed on every shore,
    we pray for the Church throughout the world:
    for the ancient and long-established Churches,
    for the young and vigorous Churches,
    for Churches under the shadow of persecution,
    for weary Churches where the fever of love has cooled.
Grant to all the joy and power of faith.

    Silence

Lord of all truth and wisdom,
    in every generation you have raised up people
    to lead your Church:
    Patriarchs and Prophets, Evangelists and Apostles.
We pray for those who serve your Church today: _____

    Silence

Creator and giver of every good and perfect gift,
    we pray for people everywhere:
    for farmers and factory workers,
    for artists and artisans,
    for secretaries and nurses,
    for doctors and lawyers,
    for managers and storekeepers,
    for teachers and students,
    for _____,
    for mothers and fathers, husbands and wives, sisters and brothers.
Grant that we may all receive from you the strength to do
    our work and by your grace make it useful to others.

Silence

Author of all peace and justice,
 we pray for our nation and those who lead it: _____;
 We pray for those who lead our state/province
  and our city: _____;
May they all be filled with a sense of dedication
 to the welfare of our land and people.

Silence

Giver of mercies and God of all consolation,
 we pray for all those who are weighed down by any sadness
  or tragedy.
 Grant to those who despair the hope of the Gospel.
 Grant to those who live in fear confidence in your strength.
 Grant to those who are bored a sense of your glory.
We remember particularly: _____.

7. The Lord's Prayer

All these mercies we ask in the name of our Lord Jesus, who taught us to pray with the confidence of children.

We therefore dare to say (sing):

ICET   LUTHERAN BOOK OF WORSHIP, 1978

Our Fa-ther in heav-en, hal-lowed be your name,

8. Benediction

The grace of our Lord Jesus Christ,
    the love of God,
        and the communion of the Holy Spirit be with you all.

Amen.

The service may end with a hymn and/or the exchange of a sign of peace. This sign may be a handshake, embrace, or whatever is considered a suitable means of expressing the communion of those present.

Brief Order of Prayer

All stand as the leader enters and invites the response of the congregation.

1. Opening

Give thanks to the Lord for he is good.

For his love endures for ever.

Glory to the Father, and to the Son, and to the Holy Spirit.

as it was in the beginning, is now, and will be for ever. Amen.

2. Hymn

The appropriate stanza of the following hymn is sung:

stanza 1—morning
stanza 2—afternoon
stanzas 3–4—evening

Lord of All Hopefulness

Jan Struther, 1901–1953

SLANE 10.11.11.12
Irish Folk Tune

1. Lord of all hopefulness, Lord of all joy,
Whose trust, ever childlike, no cares could destroy:
Be there at our waking, and give us, we pray,
Your bliss in our hearts, Lord, at the break of the day.

2. Lord of all eagerness, Lord of all faith,
Whose strong hands were skilled at the plane and the lathe:
Be there at our labors, and give us, we pray,
Your strength in our hearts, Lord, at the noon of the day.

3. Lord of all kindliness, Lord of all grace,
Your hands swift to welcome, your arms to embrace:
Be there at our homing, and give us, we pray,
Your love in our hearts, Lord, at the eve of the day.

4. Lord of all gentleness, Lord of all calm,
Whose voice is contentment, whose presence is balm:
Be there at our sleeping, and give us, we pray,
Your peace in our hearts, Lord, at the end of the day.

3. Psalms

One or more psalms and canticles may be sung or said, chosen according to the time of day. These may be found in the services for Morning Prayer and Evening Prayer and in the Appendix.

All may be seated.

4. Reading

A lesson from Scripture is read. Before doing so, the reader may say:

A reading (lesson) from _____.

After the reading, the reader may say:

The Word of the Lord.

Thanks be to God.

Silence after the reading is recommended.

5. Prayer

All may stand. The leader says the appropriate prayer.

<u>Morning</u>

Lord,
as this new day comes to life,
direct our thoughts, words, and deeds
    to the knowledge of Christ.
As we experience in our lives the pattern of his cross,
may we also know the promise of his resurrection.
Unite our every aspiration to his
that this day may be a pleasing offering to you,
made in Spirit and in truth.

We ask this in Jesus' name,
who lives and reigns with you and the Holy Spirit,
one God, for ever and ever.

Amen.

Afternoon

God of peace,
through this pause from the day's activities
lift our hearts to knowledge of you.
Bind us more deeply to doing your will
and refresh us with the presence of your Spirit.

We ask this through Christ, your Son,
who lives and reigns with you and the same Holy Spirit,
one God, for ever and ever.

Amen.

Evening

God of all consolation,
with the coming of the evening shadows
renew our trust in the presence of your Son.
As we have asked you to unite the day's work with his
    unique offering,
so make perfect this evening sacrifice of praise.

We ask this in his name, Jesus Christ,
who lives and reigns with you and the Holy Spirit,
one God, for ever and ever.

Amen.

Night

Father,
the darkness now separates us from the day's striving.
As our bodies rest under the sign of your protection,
open our hearts more deeply to your mysterious designs.
So may your name be praised,
in our sleeping and in our waking.

We ask this in Jesus' name,
who lives and reigns with you and the Holy Spirit,
one God, for ever and ever.

Amen.

6. The Lord's Prayer

And now let us pray with confidence,
    as Christ our Lord asked:

ICET   LUTHERAN BOOK OF WORSHIP, 1978

Our Father in heaven, hallowed be your name,

7. Blessing

Evening Prayer

The service may begin with the light service and hymn or with psalmody as below. If the light service and hymn are omitted the psalmody may be introduced by a suitable call to worship such as the sentences from 2 Corinthians in the light service.

1. Light Service

All may stand.

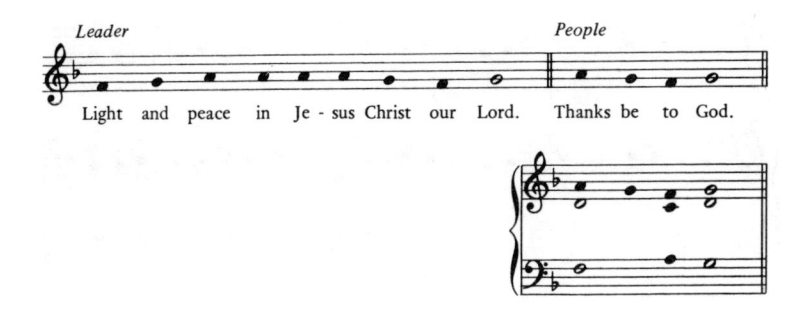

Leader: Light and peace in Jesus Christ our Lord.
People: Thanks be to God.

It is not ourselves that we proclaim; we proclaim Christ Jesus as Lord, and ourselves as your servants, for Jesus' sake. For the same God who said, "Out of darkness let light shine," has caused his light to shine within us, to give the light of revelation—the revelation of the glory of God in the face of Jesus Christ. (2 Corinthians 4:5–6)

Let us pray.

Almighty God,
we give you thanks for surrounding us, as daylight fades, with the brightness of the vesper light; and we implore you of your great mercy that, as you enfold us with the radiance of this light, so you would shine into our hearts the brightness of your Holy Spirit; through Jesus Christ our Lord.

Amen.

2. Hymn

As the hymn is sung or said, candles are lighted along with other necessary illumination.

O Gracious Light
Phos hilaron

Tone I, Introit Form

1. O gracious Light, pure brightness of the everliving Father in heaven, O Jesus Christ, holy and blessed! 2. Now as we come to the

setting of the sun, and our eyes behold the vesper light,

we sing your/thy praises, O God: Father, Son, and Holy Spirit.

3. You are/Thou art worthy at all times to be praised by happy voices,

O Son of God, O Giver of life, and to be glorified

through all the worlds.

O Gracious Light
Phos hilaron

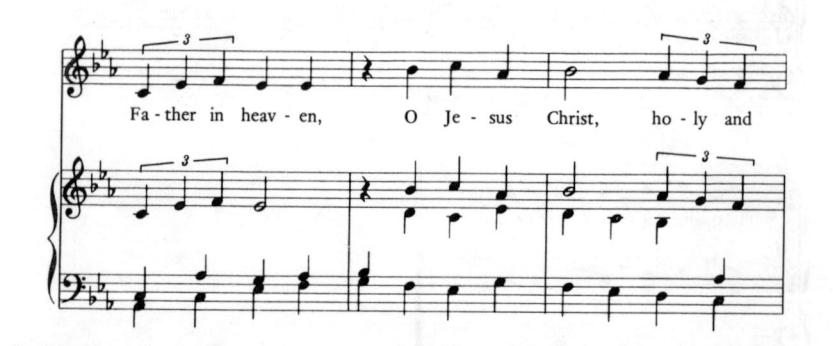

Copyright, 1978 by The Church Pension Fund.

Ronald Arnatt

1. O gracious Light, pure brightness of the ever-living Father in heaven, O Jesus Christ, holy and

bless - ed!
2. Now as we come to the set - ting of the sun,
and our eyes be - hold the ves - per light,
We sing your
thy
prai - ses, O God:
Fa - ther, Son, and Ho - ly Spir - it:

3. You are wor-thy at all times to be praised by hap-py
Thou art
voi - ces, O Son of God, O Giv-er of life, and to be
glo - ri - fied through all the worlds.

3. Psalms

As the traditional evening psalm of repentance, psalm 141 is normally used. Incense or some other symbol of penitence and self-offering may be used as the psalm is sung. If incense is used, it may simply be burned or it may be used to incense the other liturgical symbols, including leader and congregation.

Psalm 141

Antiphon:

THE GRAIL
Robert J. Batastini

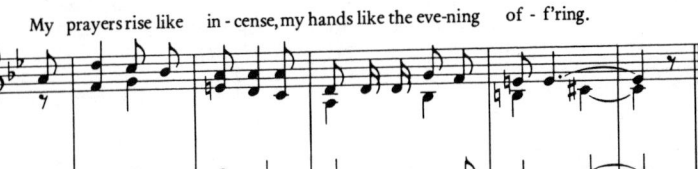

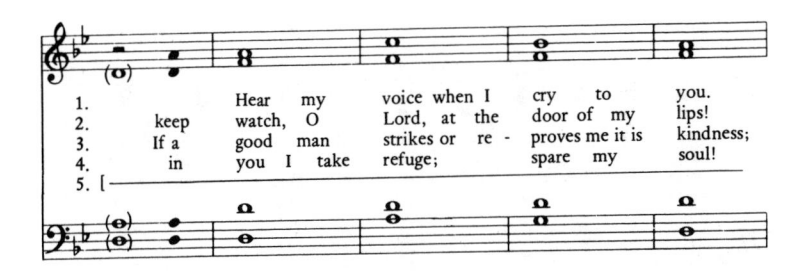

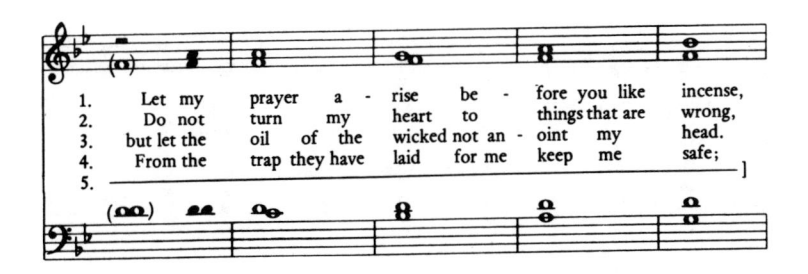

My prayers rise like in-cense, my hands like the eve-ning of-f'ring.

Joseph Gelineau

1. I have called to you, Lord; hasten to help me!
2. Set, O Lord, a guard over my mouth;
3. Never al-low me to share in their feasting.
4. To you, Lord God, my eyes are turned;
5. Give praise to the Father, the Son and Holy Spirit,

1. Hear my voice when I cry to you.
2. keep watch, O Lord, at the door of my lips!
3. If a good man strikes or re-proves me it is kindness;
4. in you I take refuge; spare my soul!
5. [

1. Let my prayer a-rise be-fore you like incense,
2. Do not turn my heart to things that are wrong,
3. but let the oil of the wicked not an-oint my head.
4. From the trap they have laid for me keep me safe;
5.]

43

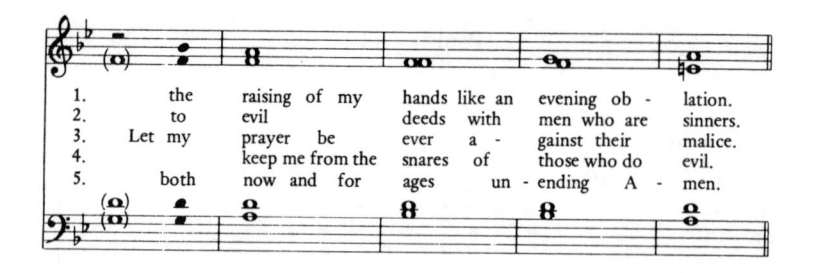

1.	the	raising of my	hands like an	evening ob -	lation.
2.	to	evil	deeds with	men who are	sinners.
3.	Let my	prayer be	ever a -	gainst their	malice.
4.		keep me from the	snares of	those who do	evil.
5.	both	now and for	ages un -	ending A -	men.

Pause for silent prayer. The following is then said by the leader, in unison, or read silently.

Lord,

from the rising of the sun to its setting your name is worthy of all praise. Let our prayer come like incense before you. May the lifting up of our hands be as an evening sacrifice acceptable to you, Lord our God.

Psalm 121

I to the Hills Will Lift My Eyes
DUNDEE (FRENCH) C.M.

From Psalm 121
The Psalter; alt., 1972

Scottish Psalter, 1615

1. I to the hills will lift my eyes; From whence shall come our aid? Our help is from
2. He will not let your foot be moved, Your guard - ian nev - er sleeps; With watch - ful and
3. Your faith - ful keep - er is the Lord, Your Shel - ter and your Shade; 'Neath sun or moon,
4. From e - vil he will keep you safe, For you he will pro - vide; Your go - ing out,

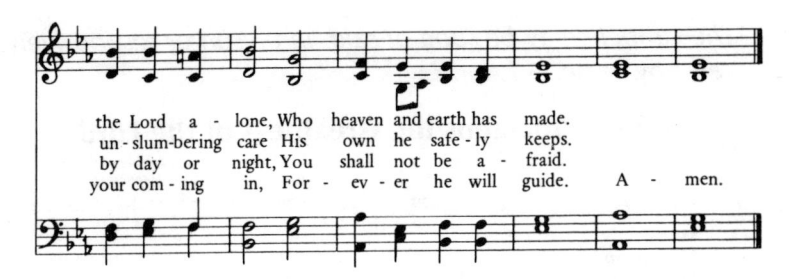

```
the Lord a - lone, Who heaven and earth has made.
un-slum-bering care His own he safe-ly keeps.
by day or night, You shall not be a - fraid.
your com - ing in, For - ev - er he will guide. A - men.
```

Pause for silent prayer. The following is then said by the leader, in unison, or read silently.

Lord,
in creation you have revealed your awesome power, and in redemption you reveal your relentless love. Through your vigilance by night and by day, teach us more intimately of your power and your love.

Other appropriate psalms may be used. After the psalmody, all may be seated.

4. Reading

A lesson from Scripture is read. Before doing so, the reader may say:

A reading (lesson) from ──────.

After the reading, the reader may say:

The Word of the Lord.

Thanks be to God.

Silence after the reading is recommended. A brief homily may also be given.

5. Canticle of Mary (Luke 1:46–55)

The canticle may be sung or said, in unison or responsively, verse by verse. All stand.

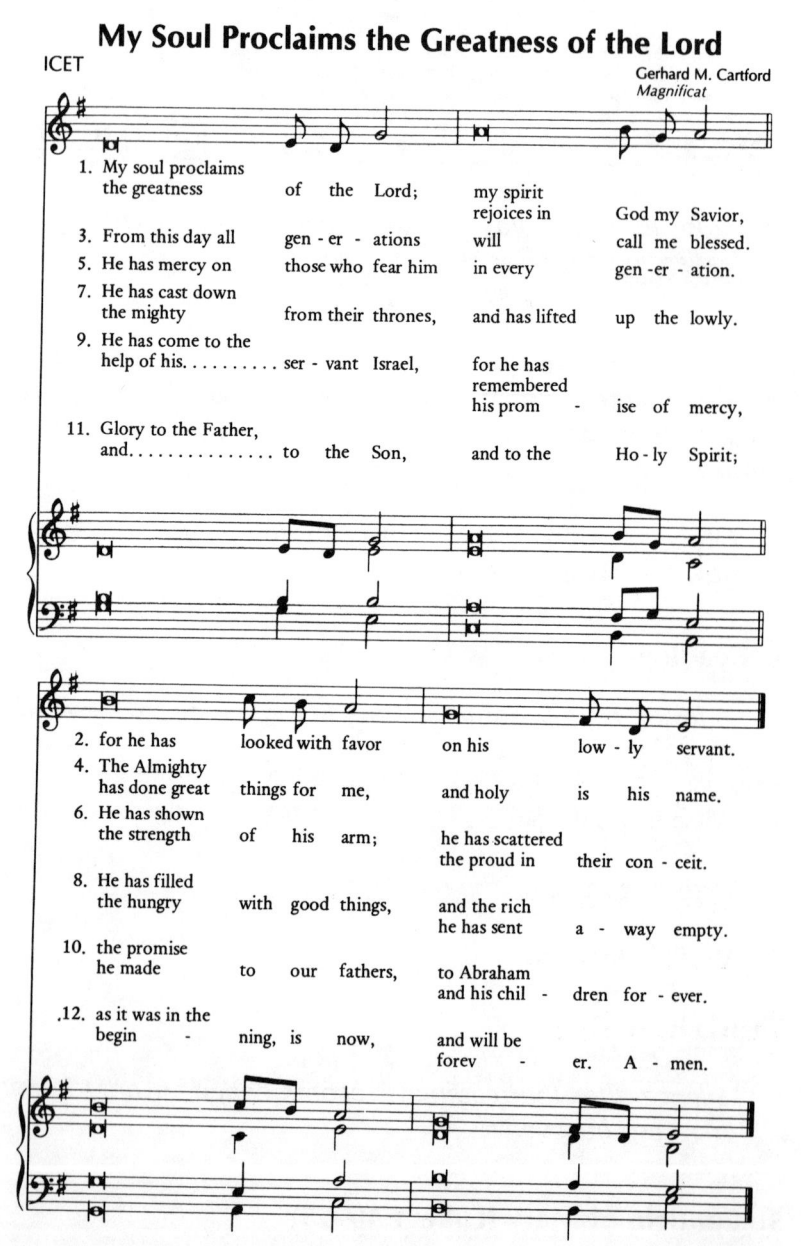

My Soul Proclaims the Greatness of the Lord

ICET

Gerhard M. Cartford
Magnificat

1. My soul proclaims the greatness of the Lord; my spirit rejoices in God my Savior,
2. for he has looked with favor on his lowly servant.
3. From this day all generations will call me blessed.
4. The Almighty has done great things for me, and holy is his name.
5. He has mercy on those who fear him in every generation.
6. He has shown the strength of his arm; he has scattered the proud in their conceit.
7. He has cast down the mighty from their thrones, and has lifted up the lowly.
8. He has filled the hungry with good things, and the rich he has sent away empty.
9. He has come to the help of his servant Israel, for he has remembered his promise of mercy,
10. the promise he made to our fathers, to Abraham and his children forever.
11. Glory to the Father, and to the Son, and to the Holy Spirit;
12. as it was in the beginning, is now, and will be forever. Amen.

6. Prayers of Intercession

The intercessions may be offered in these or similar words. Names of particular Churches, pastors, bishops, countries, and civil leaders may be supplied as appropriate. The versicle and response below may be sung or said. All remain standing.

Let us pray to the Lord.

Lord, have mer - cy.

In peace, let us pray to the Lord.

Lord, have mercy.

For God's holy Church, that it may be filled with truth and love, and be found without fault at the day of his coming, let us pray to the Lord.

Lord, have mercy.

For the ministers of the Church (especially _____), that they may be faithful to the Gospel and worthy servants of the people of God, let us pray to the Lord.

Lord, have mercy.

For all who fear God and believe in the Lord Jesus, that our divisions may cease, and that all may be one, as he wills, let us pray to the Lord.

Lord, have mercy.

For the mission of the Church, that in faithful witness it may preach the Gospel to the ends of the earth, let us pray to the Lord.

Lord, have mercy.

For those who do not yet believe, and for those who have lost their faith, that they may receive the light of the Gospel, let us pray to the Lord.

Lord, have mercy.

For the peace of the world, that respect and understanding may grow among nations and peoples, let us pray to the Lord.

Lord, have mercy.

For those in positions of public trust (especially _____), that they may serve justice and truth, and promote the dignity and freedom of every person, let us pray to the Lord.

Lord, have mercy.

For our families and all those who are dear to us; for the aged and for the young that they may have a future to hope in, let us pray to the Lord.

Lord, have mercy.

For the poor, the persecuted, the sick, and all who suffer; for refugees, prisoners, and all who are in danger, that they may be relieved and protected, let us pray to the Lord.

Lord have mercy.

For our enemies, and those who wish us harm; and for all whom we have injured or offended, let us pray to the Lord.

Lord, have mercy.

Intercessions may be offered by anyone present.

For _____, let us pray to the Lord.

Lord, have mercy.

The intercessions are concluded with a prayer, or the following doxology:

For yours is the majesty, O Father, Son, and Holy Spirit; yours is the kingdom and the power and the glory, now and for ever.

Amen.

7. The Lord's Prayer

With the confidence of children we dare to sing (say):

ICET LUTHERAN BOOK OF WORSHIP, 1978

Our Father in heaven, hallowed be your name, your kingdom come, your will be done, on earth as in heaven. Give us today our

dai - ly bread. For - give us our sins as
we for - give those who sin a - gainst us. Save us from the
time of tri - al and de - liv - er us from e - vil.

For the king-dom, the pow'r, and the glo-ry are yours, now and for-ev-er. A-men.

8. Benediction

The Lord bless you and keep you: the Lord make his face to shine upon you and be gracious to you: the Lord lift up his countenance upon you and give you peace.

Amen.

> *The service may end with a hymn and/or the exchange of a sign of peace. This sign may be a handshake, embrace, or whatever is considered a suitable means of expressing the communion of those present.*

Appendix

I. Psalms

A. Morning

Psalm 145

O Lord, You Are Our God and King
DUKE STREET L.M.

From Psalm 145:1–7
The Psalter, 1912; alt., 1972

John Hatton, 1793

1. O Lord, you are our God and king, And we will ev - er bless your name; We will ex - tol you
2. The Lord is great - ly to be praised; His great - ness is be - yond our thought; From age to age the
3. Up - on your glo - rious maj - es - ty And won - drous works our minds shall dwell; Your deeds shall fill the
4. Your match - less good - ness and your grace Your peo - ple shall com - mem - o - rate, And all your truth and

53

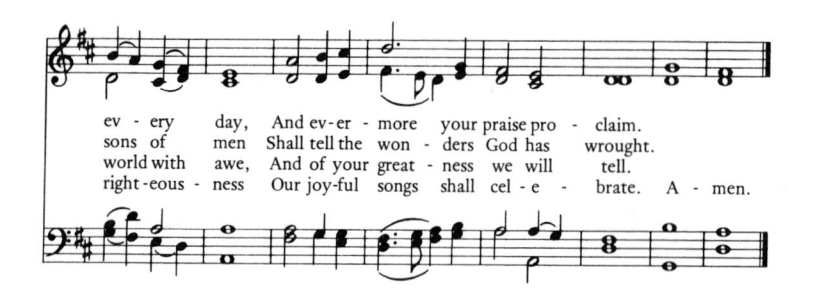

ev - ery day, And ev-er-more your praise pro - claim.
sons of men Shall tell the won - ders God has wrought.
world with awe, And of your great - ness we will tell.
right-eous - ness Our joy-ful songs shall cel - e - brate. A - men.

Pause for silent prayer. The following is then said by the leader, in unison, or read silently.

Lord,
may we proclaim your faithfulness in all we say and do, that generations to come may acknowledge you as their maker, and Jesus, your Son, as their redeemer.

Psalm 148

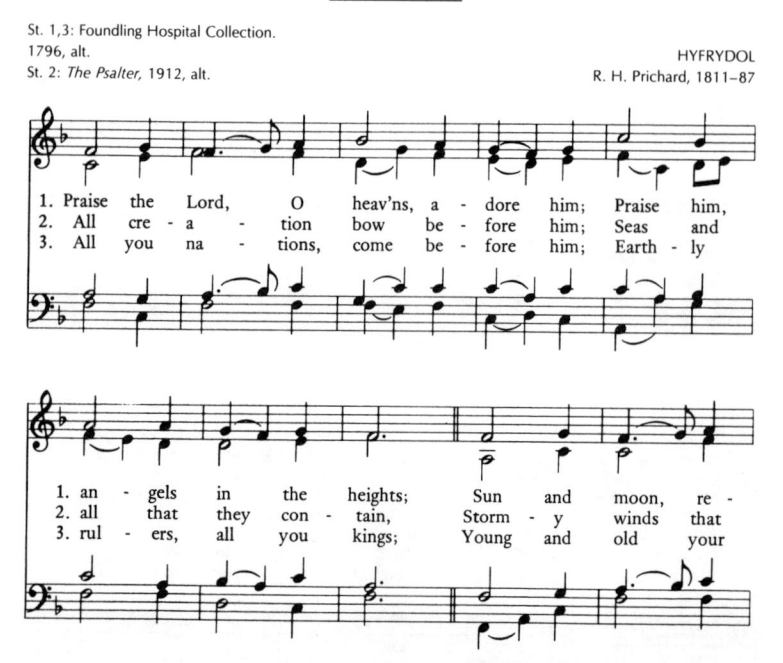

St. 1,3: Foundling Hospital Collection.
1796, alt.
St. 2: *The Psalter,* 1912, alt.

HYFRYDOL
R. H. Prichard, 1811–87

1. Praise the Lord, O heav'ns, a - dore him; Praise him,
2. All cre - a - tion bow be - fore him; Seas and
3. All you na - tions, come be - fore him; Earth - ly

1. an - gels in the heights; Sun and moon, re -
2. all that they con - tain, Storm - y winds that
3. rul - ers, all you kings; Young and old your

1. joice be - fore him; Praise him, shin - ing stars of light.
2. do his pleas - ure, Hail and light - ning, snow and rain.
3. praise ex - press - ing, Join - ing all cre - a - ted things.

Pause for silent prayer. The following is then said by the leader, in unison, or read silently.

Lord,
help us to raise our song of praise in union with all creation.
May all our desires be directed to you and our actions, to your glory.

Psalm 150

THE GRAIL   A. G. Murray, O.S.B.

Let eve - ry-thing that lives praise the Lord.

Joseph Gelineau

Psalm   (Mode: Fah. Tonic: E♭)

1. Praise God in his ho - ly place,
2. O praise him with sound of trumpet,
3. O praise him with re - sounding cymbals,
4. Give praise to the Father Al - mighty, to his

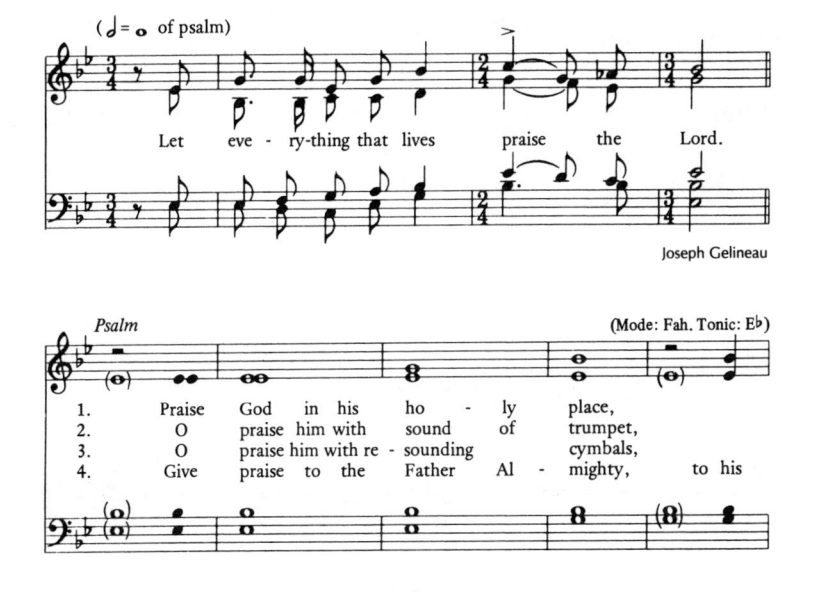

55

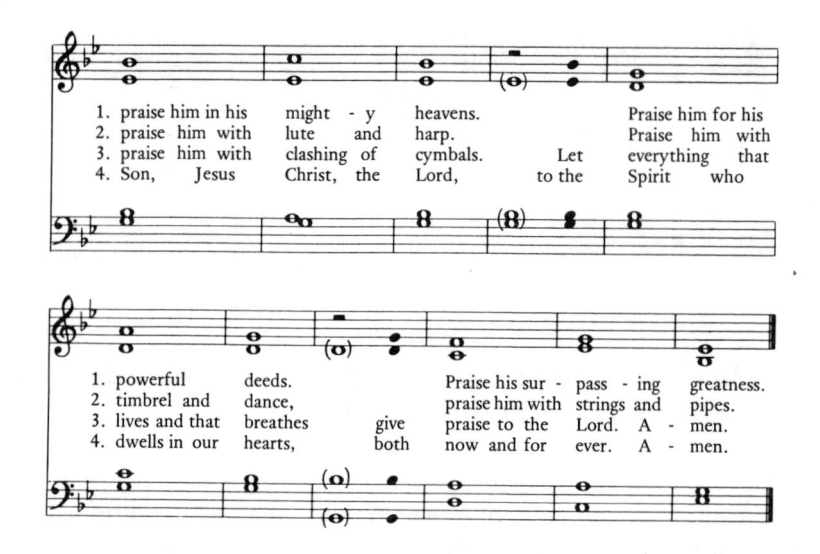

1. praise him in his might-y heavens. Praise him for his powerful deeds. Praise his sur-pass-ing greatness.
2. praise him with lute and harp. Praise him with timbrel and dance, praise him with strings and pipes.
3. praise him with clashing of cymbals. Let everything that lives and that breathes give praise to the Lord. A-men.
4. Son, Jesus Christ, the Lord, to the Spirit who dwells in our hearts, both now and for ever. A-men.

Pause for silent prayer. The following is then said by the leader, in unison, or read silently.

Lord,
in all things you draw us back to yourself and reveal your loving plan.
Open our hearts to do your will and help us to rejoice in the awareness of your presence.

Amen.

B. Afternoon

Psalm 126

THE GRAIL   Joseph Gelineau

Unison only Those who sow in tears and sor-row, one day will reap with joy.

Psalm (Mode: Me. Tonic: F♯)

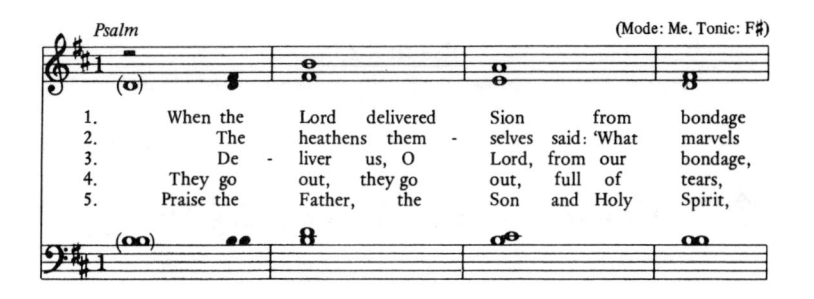

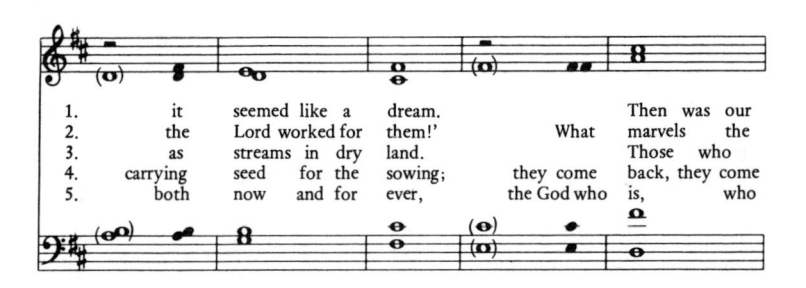

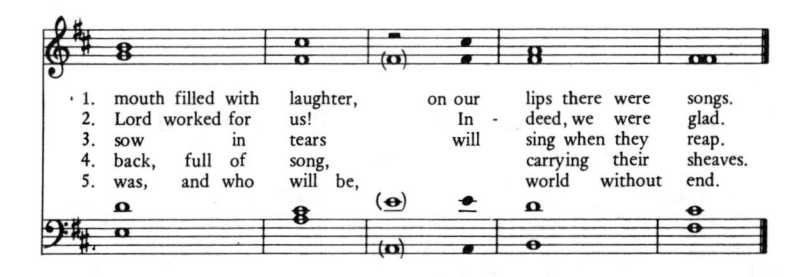

1. When the Lord delivered Sion from bondage it seemed like a dream. Then was our mouth filled with laughter, on our lips there were songs.
2. The heathens them-selves said: 'What marvels the Lord worked for them!' What marvels the Lord worked for us! In-deed, we were glad.
3. De-liver us, O Lord, from our bondage, as streams in dry land. Those who sow in tears will sing when they reap.
4. They go out, they go out, full of tears, carrying seed for the sowing; they come back, they come back, full of song, carrying their sheaves.
5. Praise the Father, the Son and Holy Spirit, both now and for ever, the God who is, who was, and who will be, world without end.

Pause for silent prayer. The following is then said by the leader, in unison, or read silently.

Lord,
give us the eyes of faith, that we may perceive your hidden ways and give us the hope to sustain us, until your designs are brought to completion.

Psalm 123

ICEL — C. Alexander Peloquin

Our eyes are fixed on the Lord, pleading for his mercy.

C. A. P.
(Mode: Te. Tonic: A)

THE GRAIL — Joseph Gelineau

1. To you have I lifted up my eyes, you who dwell in the heavens; my eyes, like the eyes of slaves on the hand of their lords.
2. Like the eyes of a servant on the hand of her mistress, so our eyes are on the Lord our God till he show us his mercy.
3. Have mercy on us, Lord,/ have mercy. We are filled with contempt. Indeed all too full is our soul with the scorn of the rich, / with the proud man's disdain. }*
4. Praise the Father, the Son, and Holy Spirit, both now and for ever, the God who is, who was, and who will be, world without end.

*Repeat the final musical phrase for the additional text.

Pause for silent prayer. The following is then said by the leader, in unison, or read silently.

Lord,
your mercy is the only remedy for our weakness.
Help us to hold to you unswervingly and to await patiently your help.

C. Evening

Psalm 23

The Lord's My Shepherd

Text; *Psalter,* Edinburgh, 1650

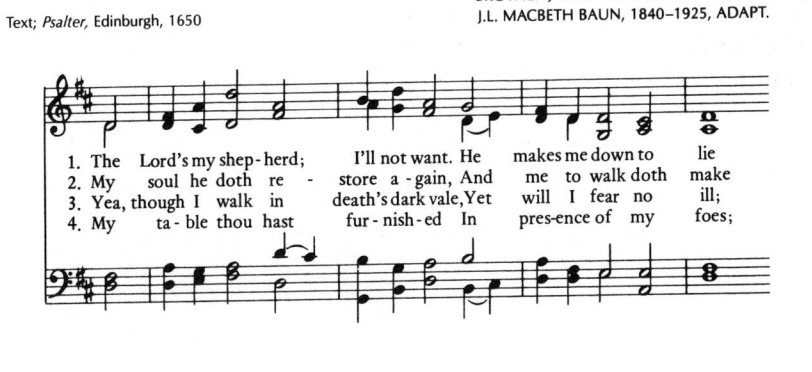

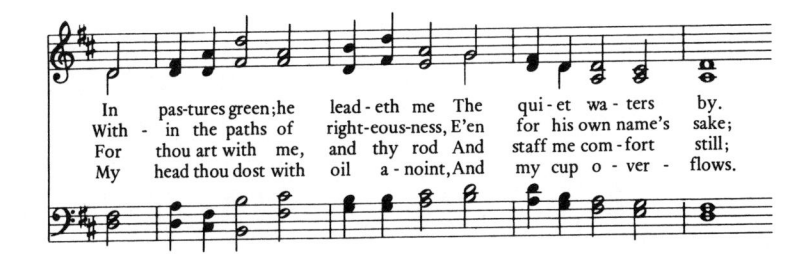

BROTHER JAMES' AIR 86.86.86
J.L. MACBETH BAUN, 1840–1925, ADAPT.

1. The Lord's my shep-herd; I'll not want. He makes me down to lie
   In pas-tures green; he lead-eth me The qui-et wa-ters by.
2. My soul he doth re - store a-gain, And me to walk doth make
   With - in the paths of right-eous-ness, E'en for his own name's sake;
3. Yea, though I walk in death's dark vale, Yet will I fear no ill;
   For thou art with me, and thy rod And staff me com-fort still;
4. My ta-ble thou hast fur-nish-ed In pres-ence of my foes;
   My head thou dost with oil a-noint, And my cup o-ver-flows.

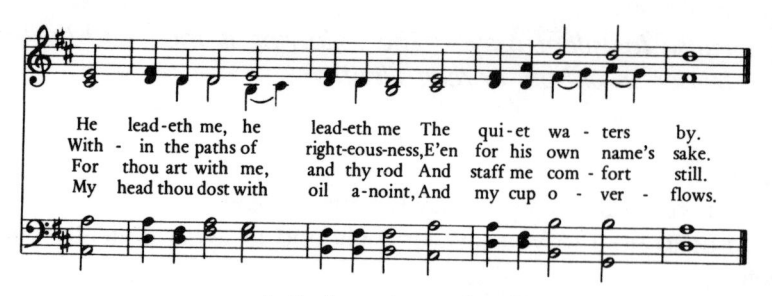

He	lead-eth me, he	lead-eth me The	qui-et wa - ters by.
With-	in the paths of	right-eous-ness, E'en	for his own name's sake.
For	thou art with me,	and thy rod And	staff me com - fort still.
My	head thou dost with	oil a-noint, And	my cup o - ver - flows.

5. Goodness and mercy all my life
Shall surely follow me,
And in God's house forevermore
My dwelling-place shall be.

Pause for silent prayer. The following is then said by the leader, in unison, or read silently.

Lord Jesus Christ,
shepherd of your Church, you give us new birth in the waters of baptism, anoint us with saving oil, and call us to salvation at your table. Dispel the terrors of death and the darkness of error. Lead your people along safe paths, that they may rest securely in you and live for ever in your Father's house.

II. Supplemental List of Psalms, Lessons, and Hymns

A. Psalms

Morning:	*Pss. 5, 24, 36, 51, 63, 67, 100*
Afternoon:	*Pss. 19B, 25:12–22, 69, 80, 119:97–104, 125, 127*
Evening:	*Pss. 4, 91, 111, 113, 119:105–112, 122, 130, 132, 134*
Advent:	*Pss. 24, 25, 46, 50, 75, 80, 85, 132*
Christmas Season:	*Pss. 2, 19, 24, 45, 46, 72, 89, 96, 97, 98, 110*
Lent:	*Pss. 27, 30, 32, 44, 51, 84, 91, 102, 103, 130*
Easter Season:	*Pss. 3, 16, 23, 24, 29, 30, 33, 66, 68, 104, 110, 114, 118*
National Holiday:	*Pss. 65, 72, 145*
Unity:	*Pss. 122, 133*
Peace:	*Ps. 85*

B. Lessons

Advent:	*Isaiah*
Christmas Season:	*I John; Chapters 1–2 of Matthew and Luke*
Lent:	*Exodus; Jeremiah; Mark; Hebrews*
Easter Season:	*Acts; I Peter; Revelation*
National Holiday:	*Deuteronomy 8:1–20; Jeremiah 29:4–14; Matthew 6:25–33; Mark 12:13–17; Luke 17:11–19; Romans 13:1–10*
Unity:	*John 17:15–23; Ephesians 4:1–6*
Peace:	*Micah 4:1–5; Colossians 3:12–15; John 15:9–12*

C. Hymns

Morning:	"Christ, Whose Glory Fills the Skies"
	"This Day God Gives Me"

Afternoon: "Son of God, Eternal Savior"
"For the Beauty of the Earth"

Evening: "Now All the Woods Are Sleeping"
"The Day You Gave Us, Lord, Has Ended"
"Through the Night of Doubt and Sorrow"
"God, Who Made the Earth and Heaven"

General: "The Church's One Foundation"
"Where Cross the Crowded Ways of Life"
"Praise to the Lord, the Almighty"

acknowledgements continued

London, 1963. Available in North America through the Paulist Press, and Collins & World. Response for Psalm 123 from LECTIONARY FOR MASS © 1969, International Committee on English in the Liturgy, Inc. (ICEL); psalm prayers for Psalm 141 and Psalm 23 from THE LITURGY OF THE HOURS © 1974, ICEL. All rights reserved. Psalms 145, 146, 147, 148, and 150 in Morning Prayer, Scripture and prayers in Evening Light Service, and Benediction in Evening Prayer from BOOK OF COMMON PRAYER, Church Hymnal Corporation, New York. "Lord of All Hopefulness" from ENLARGED SONGS OF PRAISE by permission of Oxford University Press. "O Come and Sing Unto the Lord," "I to the Hills Will Lift My Eyes," "O Lord You Are Our God and King" reproduced from THE WORSHIPBOOK—SERVICES AND HYMNS © 1970, 1972, the Westminster Press. Reproduced by permission. Prayers of Intercession reprinted from MORNING PRAISE AND EVENSONG with permission of Fides/Claretian, 221 W. Madison St., Chicago, IL 60606. MUSIC: Musical setting of the Invitatory ("Light and Peace") and the two settings of "O Gracious Light" (Tone I and setting by Ronald Arnatt) in Evening Prayer from THE BOOK OF CANTICLES, copyright, The Church Pension Fund. Used by permission. Musical settings of the Lord's Prayer, Canticle of Zechariah, and Canticle of Mary from LUTHERAN BOOK OF WORSHIP, Copyright 1978, by permission of Augsburg Publishing House. Musical setting of "The Lord's My Shepherd" (Brother James' Air) by permission of Oxford University Press. SLANE harmonization by Carlton R. Young. Copyright © 1964 by Abingdon Press. Used by permission. Music for the antiphons for Psalms 123 and 141 from WORSHIP II Copyright © 1975 G.I.A. Publications, Inc. All rights reserved. Music for Psalms 123, 126, 141, and 150 and music for antiphons for Psalms 126 and 150 by Joseph Gelineau, copyright © 1963 by The Grail (England). All rights reserved.